Dogs: 101 AMAZING DOG FUN FACTS AND TRIVIA FOR KIDS

Learn To Love and Train The Perfect Dog (WITH 40+ PHOTOS!)

© Copyright 2018 by Cesar Dunbar – All rights reserved.

In no way is it legal to reproduce, duplicate, or transmit any part of this document in either electronic means or in printed format. Recording of this publication is strictly prohibited and any storage of this document is not allowed unless with written permission from the publisher.

The information provided herein is stated to be truthful and consistent, in that any liability, in terms of inattention or otherwise, by any usage or abuse of any policies, processes, or directions contained within is the solitary and utter responsibility of the recipient reader. Under no circumstances will any legal responsibility or blame be held against the author for any reparation, damages, or monetary loss due to the information herein, either directly or indirectly.

The information herein is offered for informational purposes solely, and is universal as so. The presentation of the information is without contract or any type of guarantee assurance.

Medical Disclaimer: The ideas and suggestions contained in this book are not intended as a substitute for consulting with your veterinary physician. All matters regarding your dog's health require medical supervision.

Legal Disclaimer: all photos used in this book are licensed for commercial use or in the public domain.

Table of Contents

INTRODUCTION 4
101 DOG FACTS & TRIVIA 11
DOG QUIZ 116
DOG QUIZ ANSWERS 120
BONUS CHAPTER: HOW TO CHOOSE THE RIGHT DOG 124
FINAL THOUGHTS 136
DID YOU LIKE THIS BOOK? 140
BY THE SAME AUTHOR 144

INTRODUCTION

Did you know that puppies gain half their body weight in their first four-to-five months?

After that, it takes about one more year to grow to their full adult dog body weight.

I'm a bit of sucker for dog facts like these...

Do you ever get that question: "*Are you a dog person or a cat person?*"

Well, for me, there's no doubt: **I love dogs**!

What about you?

If you are also crazy about dogs, then *this* is the book for you. I am going to share with you all that I know about dogs.

This book is full of **fun dog facts** and **trivia** that will:

- warm your heart
- make you smile, *and*
- teach you a little something about what it takes to raise and train a dog with love and care.

Moreover, this book contains more than 40 **beautiful photos** of the <u>**cutest dogs**</u> you've ever seen!

Doesn't she look cute? Don't you just want to take her home, right NOW?

At the end, there's a **'Dog Quiz'** with 21 questions to test your newly gained puppy knowledge.

Here are some of the questions you will be able to answer at the end of this book:

- Who can hear better: dogs or humans?
- Why do Poodles have such funny haircuts?

- What was the main ingredient in 'puppy water', a 17th century cosmetic?
- What is the smallest dog breed in the world?
- Who mature faster: smaller or larger dog breeds?

I hope that sparked your curiosity...

If you're the type of person that starts smiling each time you see a dog, **you've come to the right place**.

Whether you already have a dog, or simply want to learn more about these wonderful creatures: *this* is the book for you!

So, *let's dive straight in*, shall we?

Here are 101 Dog Facts and Trivia...

101 DOG FACTS & TRIVIA

1.

Dogs are able to recognize over 150 words. According to a study published in the journal *Science,* dogs' brains process words in a similar way as human brains. For example, when you say 'Good boy!' to your dog, the left and right side of the brain work together to find the word meaning. One side focuses on the word itself, the other side on the emotion (which it determines based on intonation; *how* you say the word). The reward center of the dog's brain is only activated when both sides agree the word means praise.

2.

When a puppy is born, it can't see or hear anything; it's blind and deaf. Puppies are also born without any teeth. So, the first sense a puppy experiences is touch. Therefore, when you pick up a little pup, be very gentle with it!

3.

It takes about one to two weeks for a puppy to open its eyes.

4.

By closely monitoring its tail, you can tell how a dog is feeling. If it's a big helicopter-like rotation, you're looking at a very friendly dog. However, if the tail moves up and down rapidly, in a stiff motion, the dog is excited and focused.

5.

Still having trouble figuring out what your dog's tail wagging means? Then you may want to try the 'wagometer'! This device, invented in 2003 by dog expert dr. Roger Mugford, supposedly measures whether a dog is happy, upset, or even about to attack.

6.

Every year, Rover's (the largest network of pet sitters and dog walkers in the U.S.) releases their report with most popular dog names.

Can you make a guess what the most popular names were in 2017?

According to Rover's 2017 annual report, the most popular names were Max, Charlie and

Cooper, for male dogs, and Bella, Lucy and Daisy, for female dogs.

7.

It is estimated that there are approximately 400 million dogs in the world. The United States has the highest pet dog population in the world, around 78 million. France is in second place.

8.

Have you ever wondered where the name Greyhound Bus came from?

In 1914, Carl Eric Wickman, a Swedish immigrant, began a bus service for miners. Four years later, he was running a successful transport business, owning 18 buses.

One day, the operator of one of the routes noticed the reflection of the bus in the window of a store. That reflection reminded him of a greyhound dog. He decided to use that name for this particular line. The name quickly became very popular and, eventually, the name Greyhound was applied to all buses.

9.

A dog's life is a lot shorter than a human's life. On average, a dog lives ten to fourteen years.

10.

On average, for each human baby being born, fifteen dogs are born in the United States. You don't need to be a mathematician to see that, with these birth rates, a lot of puppies may have trouble finding a home. For this reason, it is recommended that you spay or neuter your dog.

11.

Thomas Jefferson, one of the American Founding Fathers, and the third president of the United States, came up with the first dog licensing law. Can you guess why?

His sheep were being killed by dogs! He wanted to be able to contact the owners and ask for compensation.

12.

There was a Dog Tax war in New Zealand, at the end of the 19th Century.

In 1898, the Northern Māori opposed a so-called dog tax enforced by the British settlers. However, because a truce and surrender was negotiated in time, almost no shots were being fired and nobody was killed.

13.

According to a 2016 survey conducted by the Banfield pet hospital in the United Kingdom, 82% of employees feel more loyal towards a pet-friendly company.

Also, 88% of them believe that having a pet at work improves morale and 86% of employees say a pet at work reduces stress.

There is also scientific evidence that supports the claim that having a pet around at work can reduce stress and increase happiness. However, only 8% of employers in the US and the UK allow their employees to bring their pet to work...

14.

In 2014, HOWND® established the 'Bring Your Dog to Work Day', on 22 June of each year.

On this day, companies across the UK allow their employees to bring their dog to work. The purpose of this day is to raise money for charity and raise awareness for the benefits of having a dog at the workplace.

15.

Every dog sheds its fur. Through shedding, the dog replaces old hairs with new, healthy hairs. Dogs are canine, and as such, it is important that they keep warm and are protected from abrupt temperature changes. You can help you dog by regularly brushing it, in order to remove the old fur.

16.

When the city of Rome fell, dogs were neglected: the Romans had to prioritize their survival over training their dogs. Shortly after, stories of werewolves began to emerge. This can likely be attributed to abandoned dogs roaming the streets of the city in packs, terrifying the urban dwellers.

17.

The word 'werewolf' isn't Latin, though. Its origin is more recent. It is a combination of the two Old English words 'were', which means 'man', and 'wulf', which means 'wolf'.

18.

Dogs have far superior hearing than humans: they can hear four times as far as we can. Moreover, a dog's frequency range is also wider than that of humans. It can hear high pitched sounds up to 45,000 Hertz, whereas a human can only hear sounds up to 23,000 Hertz.

19.

Dogs come in all sorts and sizes. However, only one can be the largest breed: the Irish Wolfhound. However, the largest dog ever recorded was not an Irish Wolfhound. That honor goes to a Great Dane named Zeus. In 2011, he measured 44 inches tall!

20.

You can probably guess what the smallest dog breed in the world is. Hint: it fits in a lady's purse...

That's right, a Chihuahua!

The current smallest dog world record holder, according to the Guinness Book of World Records, is Milly. Indeed, a Chihuahua. She measures only 3.8 inches high!

21.

There are many stray dogs in Thailand. One of the reasons is that people get a puppy, but then abandon the dog as it grows older and is no longer cute. Another reason is that it is not common to spay or neuter dogs. Many stray dogs end up at one of the many Buddhist temples, where they are taken care of by orange-robed monks.

22.

There is archaeological evidence that dogs have been domesticated by human beings as far as 33,000 years ago. This is mostly based on genetic evidence: shortened muzzles and widening of the teeth.

Regardless of the exact date, it is clear that dogs have been man's best friend for quite some time!

23.

Dogs have three eyelids. Like us, they have an upper lid and a lower lid. However, they also have a third lid, that protects their eyes by keeping it moist.

24.

According to APPA, the American Pet Products Association, approximately 44% of all American households own a dog. And cats? That's a little less: around 35%.

25.

The Chinese Zodiac is based on a twelve-year cycle. It attributes an animal and its attributes to each year. One of the animals in the Chinese Zodiac is a Dog. It is believed that people born in the year of the Dog possess desirable traits like honesty, loyalty and responsibility.

26.

If you've ever seen a few stray dogs, you've probably noticed that they operate in a pack. When they are organized in a pack – which can consist of only two dogs –, dogs more likely to go hunting than a single dog on its own.

27.

Scientists in Croatia researched why a number of lamp posts were falling down. Their findings? Dog urine! A dog's urine contains corrosive acids, which corrodes metal. Some lamp posts were so popular with the dogs that they actually collapsed because of all the dog pee!

28.

Speaking of urine: did you know that a dog's urine is like a secret chemical messenger? When another dog smells it, it can tell whether the urinating dog is male or female, old or young, and even if it's healthy of sick!

29.

The American Kennel Club ("AKC") was founded in 1884. It was established to advance the study, breeding and maintenance of purity of thoroughbred dogs. Today, the AKC is not only the largest, but also most influential registry of purebred dogs in the United States.

30.

Every year, the AKC releases a ranking of the most popular dog breeds in the United States. In 2017, the most popular breeds (ranked 1 to 5) were: Retrievers (Labrador), German Shepherd Dogs, Retrievers (Golden), French Bulldogs, and Bulldogs.

31.

All dog breeds have pink tongues. All, but two: Shar Pei and Chow Chow. Their tongues aren't pink, but black. Whereas Shar Peis are born with a black tongue, a Chow Chow puppy's tongue is pink when its born. However, it changes into black after about 8-10 weeks. So, if this happens to your Chow Chow puppy, don't be scared! It's natural.

32.

Jeff Koons is an American artist, famous for his large-scale reproductions of mundane objects.

In 1992, Koons, created the artwork 'Puppy'. It is sculpture of a West Highland Terrier. 'Puppy' is 43 feet tall, and is made with stainless steel, soil, and covered with bedding plants.

Want to see it? Then you'll have to travel quite a bit. It is located in Spain, outside of the Guggenheim Museum in Bilbao!

33.

Alexander the Great, who conquered most of the known world in the 4th Century BC, had a dog named Peritas. According to the writer Plutarch, when Alexander's dog died, he founded a city and named it after his dog: Peritas. It is believed this city was probably in India.

34.

When countess Karlotta Leibenstein of Germany died in 1991, she left $80 million dollars to Gunther III, a German shepherd. However, the real winner here is his son, Gunther IV. He inherited his Gunther III's fortune. And thanks to the wise investments of its caretakers, his net value was estimated at a whopping $400 million in 2016!

And boy, does he live large. In 2001, he showed up in a chauffeur-driven limousine at an auction house in Italy, where he won the bid for a very rare white truffle. The winning bid? $1.1 million!

35.

Dogs cannot read clocks, but they do have a sense of time. They are able to pick up on our habits and routines. Also, according to one study, they are able to sense how much time has passed. So don't leave your dog alone for hours: it will be able to sense you've been away for a long time!

36.

The actor Josh Hutcherson, who played Peeta in 'The Hunger Games', adopted a Pit Bull puppy that had been at the shelter for almost four months. When it arrived, it had a broken leg and was missing two toes. Luckily, he got surgery before Hutcherson brought him home. The puppy's name is Driver, after the main character in the 2011 movie Drive, starring Ryan Gosling.

37.

Smaller dog breeds mature faster than larger dog breeds. Smaller breeds also live longer than larger breeds.

38.

Teddy Roosevelt, former U.S. President, owned a Bulldog named Pete. This dog was notorious for his aggression: he regularly bit visitors to the White House. According to dr. Ronnie G. Elmore, a veterinarian and expert on presidential pets, one day Pete even ripped the pants off Jules Jusserand, the French ambassador. Eventually, he was banned from the White House.

39.

The end of "A Day in the Life", a song recorded by The Beatles, contains a high-pitched whistle. Actually, it is so high that only dogs can hear it! Paul McCartney included this whistle especially for Martha, his dog.

40.

If you are a boy scout or girl scout, you can earn dog care badges. Both Boy Scouts and Girl Scouts offer merit badges for dog care and pet care.

41.

Often, feet disorders in dogs are caused by long toenails.

42.

Dogs have very powerful noses. According to scientific studies, they can even detect certain early stage illnesses in human beings, such as kung cancer. So, if your dog behaves in a strange way around you after it smelled your breath, there may be cause for concern!

43.

Every year, many dogs participate in the World's Ugliest Dog Contest. This contest has been held since the 1970s. Many participants were shelter dogs, originally. In 2018, the contest was won by Zsa Zsa, an English bulldog.

44.

Some dogs are smarter than others. Border Collies and Poodles are considered to be the most intelligent dog breeds.

45.

If some breeds are the smartest, there also have to be breeds that are considered to be the least intelligent. This dubious honor goes to the Afghan Hound and the Basenji.

46.

Most dogs have four toes on each foot. The Norwegian Lundehund, however, is the only dog with six toes on each foot.

47.

There were twelve dogs on board of the Titanic. Three survived: one Pekingese and two Pomeranians. They were all owned by First Class cabin passengers.

48.

Dogs are mentioned 41 times in the Bible. 32 times in the Old Testament and 9 times in the New Testament. In most cases, they are not described in the friendly, positive way in which we tend to see dogs nowadays. For example, in Kings, the prophet Elijah prophesizes that Ahab's wife Jezebel will be eaten by dogs after falling from the palace window.

49.

It is possible to train dogs to count. Some dogs can even solve simple math problems.

50.

There's a famous YouTube video of a dog sleeping on its side, moving its legs frantically as if it's running. It's dreaming! Although all dogs dream, puppies dream more often than adult dogs.

51.

Ever wondered why a dog's nose is so wet? There are a few reasons. First, a wet nose allows them to smell better, by making a thin layer of mucus that helps to absorb scent chemicals. Another reason why their nose is so wet is because they simply lick it so much!

52.

Dogs have about 1,700 taste buds. That is more than cats, who have about 470, but a lot less than humans, who have around 9,000 taste buds.

53.

In the U.S., dogs are as much a part of the family as any other member. 80% of dog owners even go as far as buying their dog gifts for their birthdays! Also, over 50% of dog owners include their dog's name when they sign holiday cards.

54.

'Puppy water' was once highly sought after. It was a cosmetic that was considered to help improve skin quality and remove wrinkles. The 1684 'Book of Receipts' by Mary Doggett contained a recipe for 'puppy water'. Can you guess what the main ingredient was?

Answer: puppy pee!

55.

Laika, a Russian stray, was the first living mammal in space. It didn't land on the moon, but in 1957 Laika orbited the Earth in the Sputnik spacecraft. She didn't survive the journey, unfortunately.

56.

Laika's memory lived on through her daughter, Pushinka. After mating with president John F. Kennedy's terrier, Charlie, Pushinka gave birth to four puppies.

57.

Barking is how dogs communicate. When a dog barks, there is often a stimulus, such as the postman delivering the mail, or exploding fireworks. A dog can also bark as a way of greeting, or to ask for help. If the barking is ongoing and excessive, the dog is stressed out. Try to calm it down by sitting next to, placing your hand on its back, and exerting calm energy.

58.

Not all dogs bark: the Basenji doesn't bark. Instead it can yodel!

59.

Q: Why did the dog cross the road?

A: To get to the 'barking' lot!

60.

In World War I, many soldiers lost their eyesight on the battlefield, where they had been exposed to mustard gas. Dr. Gerhard Stalling began training German Shepherds to help guide these veterans, and opened the first guide dog school in 1916. Ten year later, approximately 4,000 blind Germans had a guide dog.

61.

The first guide dog in the U.S. was called Buddy, a female German shepherd. Buddy has been trained upon the request of Frank Morris by Dorothy Eustis, an American dog breeder living in Europe. Morris took Buddy on a publicity tour upon returning to the U.S., in order to raise awareness for the needs of blind people, and how guide dogs can help.

62.

Dorothy Eustis and Frank Morris co-founded 'The Seeing Eye' in 1929, the first guide dog school for the blind in America.

63.

When they see a creature with a higher status in the pack, dogs are naturally submissive.

64.

Similar to fingerprints in humans, every dog has a unique nose print.

65.

Did you ever see the Walt Disney classic '101 Dalmatians'?

Dalmatian puppies are born completely white! They stay white for at least 10 days. Their characteristic black spots only emerge and develop as they grow older.

66.

According to estimates from ASPCA, the American Society for the Prevention of Cruelty to Animals, approximately 3.3 million dogs enter U.S. animal shelters nationwide every year. Every year, about 1.6 million dogs are adopted, but 670,000 are euthanized.

67.

Puppies spend 90% of its their first weeks sleeping. They spend the remaining 10% on eating. As they start their lives, they need a lot of rest, so their body can grow and develop. Similar to human babies, their sleeping time goes down to approximately fourteen hours per day when they are a few weeks old. An adult dog sleeps about ten hours per day.

68.

Another similarity between human babies and puppies can be found with Chihuahuas. Like babies, Chihuahuas are also born with a soft spot in the middle of their skull. The 'molera', as it is called, closes up as the puppy grows.

69.

At what point do start calling a puppy an adult dog? In general, a dog is considered an adult when it turns one year old. However, the breed greatly determines at what age an individual puppy can be considered mature. Small breeds mature faster than large breeds.

70.

Is someone in your family allergic to dogs? This doesn't have to be a problem! In this case, you will want to pick a dog that sheds less fur than the average dog, such as Poodles, Maltese or Bichons.

71.

According to legend, people in ancient China kept warm by putting Pekingese up their sleeves. For this reason, one kind of Pekingese was even referred to as 'sleeve'!

72.

A pregnant dog carries her puppies for roughly 9 weeks. That's a lot shorter than the 9 months a woman carries her baby!

73.

Depending on the breed, puppies are born in litters ranging from 2 to 16. The largest litter ever recorded was that of a Neapolitan mastiff, who gave birth to 24 (!) puppies in 2004.

74.

Dog's use their whiskers as sensing devices. It's almost a superpower! By using their whiskers, they can navigate better in the dark, because their whiskers pick up on subtle changes in air currents.

75.

One scientific study found that petting a dog and talking to it lowers blood pressure more than having a conversation with a human being.

76.

Some dogs are more kid-friendly than others. If you never want to worry about your kids playing with the dog, your best bet is getting a (Labrador or Golden) Retriever, Collie or German Shepherd. Another plus: these breeds are highly trainable! Who doesn't want to learn a dog some new tricks?

77.

Jennifer Aniston, who played 'Rachel' in the hit TV series Friends, adopted a Pitbull puppy in 2012. She had such a hard time deciding which puppy to take that she named it Sophie, after the novel 1979 'Sophie's Choice' written by William Styron. In that novel, Sophie has to make an impossible choice: which or her two children will live, and which one will not.

78.

Nobody likes a dog that just barks at anything, all the time. Luckily, you can train your dog to only bark when it's really necessary. The sooner you start training it, the better.

The key thing to keep in mind is that you shouldn't walk up to your dog each time it barks. If you do, you are – perhaps without realizing it, you just really care about your puppy! – teaching it that barking means that you show up five seconds later. This is not what you want to teach your dog!

Instead, when your puppy barks, especially if it happens often and randomly, first ask yourself: does it really need to pee, or is this false alarm? By ignoring his unnecessary barking, your dog will eventually learn to only bark when it really needs you. And you'll sleep much better as a result!

79.

Dogs are very social. In the wild, they always live in packs. In your home, you and your family are the dog's pack. Therefore, don't leave your dog alone for too long. A dog that spends a lot of time on its own can develop anxiety, stress and even depression.

80.

Bill Irwin is the first blind person who walked the Appalachian Trail, which is 2,100 miles long. He was accompanied by Orient, a German Shepherd guide dog.

81.

Similar to humans, dogs need to brush their teeth in order to prevent cavities and gum disease. However, they can't do it themselves...Brush your dog's teeth with a small, soft toothbrush every day, or at least a few times per week. Pet stores sell toothpaste for dogs. Finally, make sure to take your dog to the vet for an annual dental check-up.

82.

It is an urban legend that dogs are colorblind. Their eyes have receptors for shades of blue and yellow. However, dogs can't see red.

83.

Dogs are omnivores. This means they not only eat meat, but also grains and vegetables.

84.

When you smile at a dog, it is best to keep your mouth closed, or open it only slightly. Especially if you don't know the dog. When a dog sees you bearing your teeth when you smile, he will most likely interpret as an act of aggression.

85.

In Moscow, stray dogs can be seen riding the subway in search of food.

86.

The Alaskan Malamute is the ultimate winter dog. This breed can withstand temperatures as low as minus 70 degrees Fahrenheit!

87.

President Lyndon Johnson owned 2 beagles. Their names? 'Him' and 'Her'!

88.

According to the Guinness Book of World Records, a Bloodhound named Tigger holds the world record for 'Longest ears on a dog': his left and right ears measure 13.5 and 13.75 inches, respectively.

89.

After they've run up and down the dog park, dogs primarily cool themselves down by panting. Do dogs also sweat? Yes, but not where you may think: dogs sweat through their paws! However, sweating alone is not enough to cool them down. Through panting, a dog is able to cool down a much greater surface area.

90.

Ever heard the phrase 'the dog days of summer'? This phrase refers to the hottest days of the summer. You might think that this phrase refers to days that are so hot that even dogs are lying around, panting. However, this is not the case. The phrase goes back to the Roman era, where people believed that the dog star, Sirius, caused intense heat on the hottest summer days.

91.

Dogs bark differently around the world. Whereas they bark 'woof' in English speaking countries, they bark 'ham-ham' in Romania, 'buh-buh' in Sri Lanka, and 'gâu-gâu' in Vietnam!

92.

St. Bernard dogs are renowned mountain rescue dogs. The most successful St. Bernard was named Barry. He saved forty lives in the early 1800's!

93.

Did you ever wonder why Poodles have such funny haircuts? That haircut was originally meant to improve its ability to swim!

94.

Typically, dogs with long faces live a longer life. Dogs with flat faces, such as Bulldogs, tend to live shorter lives.

95.

The Norwegian painter Edward Munch, most known for his work 'The Scream', became a reclusive in his later years. He spent most of his time painting, only accompanied by his dogs and a servant. He would even take his dogs to the movies, and had blind faith in their judgment; if they barked during the movie, he would leave the cinema...

96.

Puppies are born with sharp little nails. However, it is best to not clip their nails until they are four to six weeks old. They only reason to start earlier is if their nails are hurting the mother.

97.

Besides guide dogs for the blind, there are also diabetic service dogs. A diabetic will still need to check his or her own blood sugar levels regularly, diabetic service dogs are not a replacement for that. However, these dogs are able to pick up on the scent that their diabetic companion's body releases when its insulin levels drop, and give him or her a warning signal.

98.

In 2014, a dog named Duke won the annual election for mayorship of Cormorant, Minnesota. He must have done a good job, because he was re-elected as mayor a few times!

99.

All dogs have amazing noses. However, did you know that Bloodhounds are able to trace a scent that is more than 300 hours old?!

100.

The painting 'Dog lying in the snow' by the German painter Franz Marc, which is on display at the Städel Museum, was voted most popular painting in 2008 by the museum's visitors. Shortly after completing this painting, Marc decides to exclusively paint animals. Why? Because, in his view, they were the only innocent creatures in a corrupt world.

101.

No success with dating? Then you may consider getting a dog! If a guy has a dog with him, his chances of getting a girl's phone number increase threefold. Don't pick just any dog, though. Reportedly, your best bet is Golden Retriever. The worst dog to attract a date is a Pit Bull.

DOG QUIZ

1. What is the smallest dog breed in the world?

2. Why did Thomas Jefferson come up with a dog licensing law?

3. Where does the name Greyhound Bus come from?

4. How many dogs are kept as pet in the United States?

5. What was the main ingredient in puppy water, a 17th century cosmetic?

6. Which dog breeds are considered to be the smartest?

7. Most dogs have four toes on each foot. Which dog breed has six toes on each foot?

8. How long does it take for a puppy to open its eyes?

9. What is a 'wagometer'?

10. Which dog breeds do not have pink tongues?

11. What is the first sense a puppy experiences?

12. What is the name of the first dog in space?

13. Why do Poodles have such funny haircuts?

14. Who can hear better: dogs or humans?

15. Are dogs vegetarians?

16. What was the name of the first guide dog in the United States?

17. Who won the World's Ugliest Dog 2018 contest?

18. What were the most popular dog names in 2017?

19. How many times are dogs mentioned in the Bible?

20. What are the most popular dog breeds in the United States?

21. Who mature faster: smaller or larger dog breeds?

DOG QUIZ ANSWERS

1. Chihuahua.

2. Because his sheep were being killed by dogs.

3. In the early 20th century, a route operator for noticed the reflection of the bus in the window of a store. That reflection reminded him of a greyhound dog. He decided to use that name for this particular line. The name quickly became very popular and, eventually, the name Greyhound was applied to all buses.

4. 78 million.

5. Puppy pee!

6. Border Collies and Poodles.

7. The Norwegian Lundehund.

8. 1-2 weeks.

9. A 'wagometer' is a device invented dr. Roger Mugford. Supposedly, it measures – based on how a dog wags its tail – whether a dog is happy, upset, or even about to attack.

10. Shar Pei and Chow Chow. Their tongues are black.

11. Touch.

12. Laika, a Russian stray.

13. That haircut was originally meant to improve their swimming abilities!

14. Dogs. They can hear four times as far as we can. There frequency range is also wider than that of humans. Dogs can hear high pitched sounds up to 45,000 Hertz, whereas a human can only hear sounds up to 23,000 Hertz.

15. No, dogs are omnivores: they eat food from animal and plant origin.

16. Buddy

17. Zsa Zsa, an English Bulldog.

18. In 2017, the most popular dog names were Max, Charlie and Cooper, for male dogs, and Bella, Lucy and Daisy, for female dogs.

19. 41.

20. In 2017, the most popular breeds were: Retrievers (Labrador), German Shepherd Dogs, Retrievers (Golden), French Bulldogs, and Bulldogs.

21. Smaller dog breeds. They also live longer.

BONUS CHAPTER: HOW TO CHOOSE THE RIGHT DOG

This is a bonus chapter from my book *'**Dog Training 101**: The Essential Guide to Raising A Happy Dog With Love. Train The Perfect Dog Through House Training, Basic Commands, Crate Training and Dog Obedience.'* Enjoy!

Dog Fun Fact: Puppies are born toothless. When they are 6–8 weeks of age, they will have developed a full set of 28 baby teeth. Shortly after, the puppy's permanent teeth will begin pushing out the milk teeth. When they are about 7 months old, a puppy will have 42 permanent teeth.

Dog Joke: Q: What do you call a dog magician? *A: A labracadabrador!*

***

Why Choose an Adult Dog?

Before we discuss breeds, let's start with the most important question: why would you choose (and train) an adult dog over a puppy?

First of all, **you give them a chance** they may not have had otherwise. Dogs are social creatures and belong in a pack. Your family could be just the pack they need!

Secondly, it's a good idea to get an older dog if you're new to the world of dogs, or aren't sure how your family and lifestyle will adapt. **Older dogs tend to be less work** (that's not to say it's all plain sailing though!) than a puppy and you can see straight away their size and temperament, so you won't get any surprises.

You can even consider a senior dog. The most neglected segment in the rescue dog world, senior dogs can be **the most rewarding companions**.

As opposed to them living out their days in a shelter or being put down, you can make the last few years of their lives extra special. They may not be as responsive as a puppy, but the saying '*you can't teach an old dog new tricks*' is simply not true!

You can, with **patience** and **persistence**.

They are a wonderful choice, if you are looking for a dog that has lower energy levels and is calm. The one thing you must be prepared for though is their shorter life span and possible expensive medical bills.

I personally have found adult dogs to be wonderful companions. If this book can inspire even just one person to adopt an older dog, then I will have done my job.

***

Be Honest About What You Seek in and Can Give to a Dog

Once you've decided that you want a dog, next you'll ask yourself the question: *what type of dog would be the best fit for me*?

If you are clear about what you seek in a dog, and what you can offer it, it will be much easier to pick the right breed. And the lucky dog that gets to come home with you will be happy too!

Choosing the right dog is so much more than simply picking the one you find the cutest, as tempting as it may be.

One of the episodes of the National Geographic's reality TV series 'Dog Whisperer' focused entirely on so-called 'wolfdogs'. A wolfdog is a hybrid between a domesticated dog and a wolf. Wolfs have fascinated mankind for thousands of years, and some people are intrigued when they see an ad for a wolf-puppy. They'd like to own a piece of nature. And as a puppy, wolfdogs look super cute. But as they grow older, the owner quickly learns that this isn't a regular dog: wolfs are predators, and it will protect what it considers as his property at all cost. What often happens, is that – instead of recognizing that the wolfdog is simply following its nature – the owner feels his pet is misbehaving. And before you know it, the wolfdog is put in a cage, or even brought to a shelter, where it's put to sleep.

The example of wolfdogs may be a bit extreme, but I hope you see my point: if you are clear about what kind of dog would be a good match with you, you are laying the foundation for a happy union. And you'll prevent a lot of potential problems and frustrations!

So, if you are low on energy, don't get a Jack Russell: they need a lot of walking.

Do you like to go out on runs or long hikes? Then don't get a pug. Pugs have less stamina than you. Also, their body temperature rises quickly and they cannot cool themselves down.

You need to carefully assess your current situation, and figure out which dog would be a good fit, based on your lifestyle. This includes being honest with yourself about what you can really give a dog.

***

How To Choose The *Right* Dog *For You*

Let's start with some questions you need to ponder, and issues you need to consider:

- **Lifestyle**. What is your lifestyle like? Do you work a lot outside the house or are you at home all day? Do you travel a lot? If you do, where will you dog stay when you're not there? Do you lead an active lifestyle or more sedentary? Do you live in the city or in the country? All of these are important factors in deciding which dog is right for you.

- **Money**. Dogs are expensive. They need food, vaccinations, and can have pricey vet bills if they get sick. Calculate how much you will spend each month so you can see if your income will easily cover the expenses of having a dog.
- **Apartment or house**. This will help you determine what size dog you can manage. You should also check to see if your apartment block will allow pets.
- **Free time**. How much time do you have spare to give your dog? Some breeds need constant attention and shouldn't be left alone.
- **Stimulation**. Some breeds are highly intelligent and active, traits that require a lot of mental stimulation and physical exercise. How much activity you can provide – both for the dog's mind and body – will help determine the breed that will be best for you.
- **Pedigree or mutt**. A pedigree has the advantage of you knowing the temperament and typical characteristics of that particular breed. A mutt can be less

predictable yet adopting or buying as an adult reduces the risk of unknown traits surfacing later.
- **Grooming**. You need to consider how much time you can commit to brushing your dog's coat. Some dogs have a huge amount of fur or even dreadlocks (think the Hungarian Puli) which need extra care and attention. Also, some breeds (such as the Bulldog) are notorious for drooling and can leave slithers of saliva here, there, and everywhere. That's not to put you off, just to warn you of the cleaning and maintenance required in taking care of a dog.

***

Key Takeaways

These are a few things you should really take a long, hard look at, to help you get an idea of what type of dog will be best for you. It may be your dream to have a husky, but if you live alone in a small apartment in a city and spend all day working outside of the house, it's not an ideal choice.

This chapter looked at some of the most important factors to consider when deciding on getting a dog.

There are several factors you need to consider before getting a dog. These include:

- looking at your lifestyle
- how much money you have to spend on a dog per month
- whether you live in an apartment or a house
- how much stimulation you can provide them
- how much free time you have
- how much grooming you want to do, and
- whether to get a pedigree or a mixed breed.

Once you have a clear idea of what type of dog would be a good match for you, you are one step closer to giving your future canine friend a new home.

Let's take a look at the different dog groups next, and learn their typical characteristics.

***

This is the end of this bonus chapter.

Want to continue reading?

Then you go to the Amazon website and search for "Dog Training 101."

Hope to see you there!

FINAL THOUGHTS

Have you ever watched South Park? If so, you may know that many episodes end with a conversation between Stan and Kyle that starts with: "*You know, I think I've learned something today.*"

Well, I hope *you* have also learned something today. And had a lot of fun in the process!

You already knew that dogs are cute.

But now you also have a better understanding of what it is like to *be* a dog.

And, if you are lucky enough to raise and train a dog of your own, you now also better understand how you can connect with your dog, and how to make sure it develops into a well-behaving canine.

Raising a dog changes your life. I really hope you get to experience this for yourself!

Let's end of a light note: *What do you call a frozen dog?*

Answer: a *pupsicle*!

Thank you again for reading this book, and I wish you (and your dog) all the best!

DID YOU LIKE THIS BOOK?

If you enjoyed this book, I would like to ask you for a favor. Please leave a review on Amazon!

Reviews are the lifeblood of independent authors. I know, you're short on time. But I would really appreciate even just a few sentences!

Your voice is important for this book to reach as many people as possible.

You can find the book by going to Amazon and:

- Checking your purchases, or
- Searching for "101 Dog Facts"

The more reviews this book gets, the more dog lovers will be able to find it and learn all these fun facts and trivia about dogs.

***

IF YOU DID NOT LIKE THIS BOOK, THEN PLEASE TELL ME! You can email me at **feedback@semsoli.com**, to share with me what you did not like. Perhaps I can change it.

A book does not have to be stagnant, in today's world. With feedback from readers like yourself, I can improve the book. So you can impact the quality of this book, and I welcome your feedback. Help make this book better for everyone!

Thank you again for reading this book and good luck with applying everything you have learned!

I'm rooting for you…

BY THE SAME AUTHOR

PUPPY TRAINING 101

THE ESSENTIAL GUIDE TO RAISING A PUPPY WITH LOVE

Train Your Puppy and Raise the Perfect Dog Through Potty Training, Housebreaking, Crate Training and Dog Obedience

CESAR DUNBAR

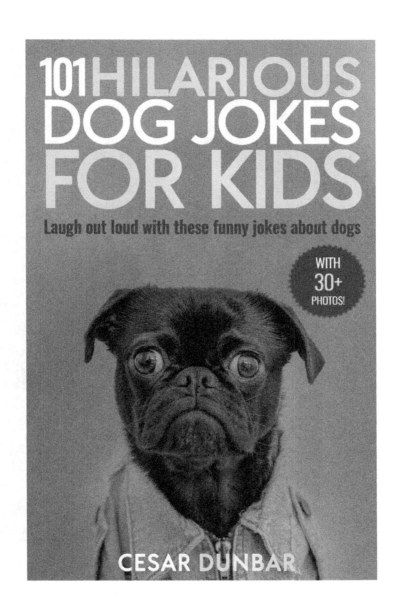

Made in the USA
Middletown, DE
10 June 2019